ANNEX ONE TO:

IN DEFENCE OF JUSTICE:

ISRAEL AND THE PALESTINIANS:
THE IDENTIFICATION OF TRUTH

Published by New Generation Publishing in 2018

First Edition

www.newgeneration-publishing.com

CONTENTS

NOTE ABOUT THE AUTHOR

Malcolm David Sinclair was called to the Bar in 1978. His professional career lasted some thirty five years during which he was involved in a number of the most serious and complex cases. He acted for both the prosecution and defence during his career. In the latter stages it was mainly as counsel for the defence. His ability as one of the top jury advocates was proven time and again by the results of cases he was involved in. He would regularly use his best endeavours to get the jury to focus upon the evidence and the evidence alone. He called upon them to dismiss from their minds matters of pure prejudice whereby the evidence became clouded over. He would often emphasize the necessity for them to bring to bear their common sense and experience of life.

He was a staunch supporter of what he considered to be the most fundamental rule of his profession as well as a rule which underpinned liberty. This rule was often more honoured by its breach than its observance by many of his colleagues. It can be stated as follows: *"A barrister must promote and protect fearlessly and by all proper and lawful means the lay client's best interests and do so without regard to his own interests or to any consequence to himself or to any other person..."*

His insistence upon upholding, not only the letter, but also the spirit of this rule would often bring him in conflict with, not only his colleagues, but also parts of the judiciary. This conflict was something throughout his professional life he regularly regretted, but took the view that it was often essential to protect liberty and to obtain a fair trial. To him, the rule had to be obeyed at all costs and must not be watered down or mere lip service paid to it. He was not prepared to 'play the game' when the liberty of an individual who, rightly or wrongly, had protested his innocence, was at stake. He was substantially critical of many in charge of his profession as he believed that their approach substantially undermined the junior Bar which, along with the jury, were the true protectors of liberty. The junior Bar was the very essence of the profession and such counsel were regularly expected to undertake highly complex tasks in the public interest for, often unknown to the public, unbelievably small rewards. However, there were a number of senior members of the judiciary who would, on occasions, compliment his advocacy and his overall approach. One typical example at the end of a trial at the Central Criminal Court (Old Bailey) during which an objection had been taken by experienced Crown Counsel to a particular method of questioning. One of England's highly respected and most experienced judges stated as follows: *"I particularly commend the examination-in-chief of the defendant by his counsel, which was the shortest one I have ever heard in this or any other court but was, nevertheless, wholly and very much to the point."*

He believed in the words 'merit' and 'integrity' as understood by ordinary decent hard working people throughout the country. He rejected that such words should be determined only by a small class of individuals not representative of the public at large. In academic terms he was one of the most highly qualified members of the Bar. Each and every qualification he possessed had been obtained on merit and on merit alone.

He was a staunch believer in the true concept of justice. He differentiated between social justice, which was a matter for the politicians; legal justice which was a matter for the courts and normative justice which was the type of justice understood by the overwhelming majority of people, both men and women, throughout the civilised world. He had one essential caveat for normative justice namely that the people had properly been made aware of the facts. He was a strong believer in the jury system, which he genuinely considered to be the bulwark of freedom, properly so called. True, a jury would not always get it right and as counsel he had little time for the guilty, but the fact remained that no better system had as yet been invented to protect the liberty of the innocent.

The same attributes which he used in his professional career he has brought to bear in his writing, particularly on the topic the subject matter of this book. It is sincerely hoped that you, the reader, will be able to glean a true understanding of some of the important issues now regularly in the public eye.

INTRODUCTION

It was my intention on writing this first Annexation to the main work **In Defence of Justice Israel and the Palestinians: The Identification of Truth** to bring the reader up to date with various events which had taken place, subsequently to the book's writing and publication. These included Operation Pillar of Defence and Operation Protective Edge. However, not only have other events superseded those operations but readers have asked me to focus on the issue 'Why, is there no peace?' using relevant events to illustrate analysis on that issue. This appeared to me to be an eminently sensible suggestion, for the reader who is interested in the specific details of the relevant military operations can readily obtain this elsewhere. I have nonetheless provided an outline of two relevant military operations to assist the reader in finding the detail of those military operations, but it is no more than the barest outline. The object of this Annex, as with the main work, is to try and make what are often said to be complex issues, readable to as many people as possible. It is not a tome or an academic thesis. This means avoiding numerous footnotes simply for the purposes of being able to cross reference each and every fact however minor and however much such a fact is common knowledge or readily available. That having been said the reader who wishes to check any matter ought to have little difficulty in cross-referencing the abundance of evidence from numerous other sources readily available to him. Accordingly, part of this Annex will provide a background to the conflict to refresh one's memory and it will then focus on matters relevant to that most important question: Why is there no true peace?

Dr. Malcolm D. Sinclair. Ph.D., LL.B. (Hons.), B.A. (Law),
Barrister. (Now retired)

PART ONE

Background

Précis dealing only with the most essential relevant matter 1948 – 1967; Basis of Palestinian Claim

The conflict between the Israelis and those who wish to be referred to as Palestinians has continued for more than seventy years. It has not been solved during this period. No politician from whichever country has been able to solve it. Indeed it is fair to say that no-one, with one possible exception[1] has got anywhere near solving it. These are not merely facts but it can properly be said that they ought to be undeniable facts. Solving does not mean a piece of paper titled 'Peace Treaty' or words to that effect. It means a deep and lasting peace supported by the majority of people on both sides.

In this Annex there is reference to Palestinians as those who wish to be called Palestinian. This has not been done out of any form of discourtesy but simply as a question of fact. There is not and never has been a sovereign state known as Palestine. It has always been an area of land within a much larger area of land. In more recent times, as a historical perspective, prior to the First World War, that larger area was an Empire: the Ottoman Empire. If people wish to refer to themselves as Palestinians that is entirely up to them. But it is essential that individuals are not mislead by wrongly assuming that there was some form of sovereign state properly referred to as Palestine and the people who call themselves Palestinians are people who themselves, or their forefathers, originate from such sovereign state. Any express assertion that individuals do originate from such a sovereign state would be wholly false, as would be any implied assertion. So what then is the present day Palestinian's claim to land which is occupied by the people of Israel and which appears to be at the root of so much bloodshed?

The claim is a simple one. Namely, that Israel 'stole' the land from, in the overwhelming majority of cases, the forefathers of the

---

[1] See Jordan below p. 30

present individuals who refer to themselves as Palestinians. There can be no doubt that a substantial number of people of the Islamic faith were either forced out of the land referred to as Palestine or left voluntarily during Israel's War of Independence in 1948. Equally, there can be no doubt that substantial numbers of Jewish people were forced out of land which they owned or occupied in countries whose principal religion was predominantly Islam during the same period. However, it is viewed one can only 'steal' land if the person you are alleged to have stolen it from has a right to the land in the first place or at the very least has a better claim to it than the alleged 'thief'.

What then is the basis for this claim of theft? For however you 'dress it up' that is the reality of the 'claim'. In the very rare and very exceptional case a descendant of an occupier during the Ottoman Empire period, it would appear, has been able to prove legal title originating from that period. In such a case he has been able to apply for an appropriate judgment in a court in Israel. However, those cases are exceedingly rare. This has not been the case when a Jewish person had been forced out of his land in a country whose main religion was that of Islam, in some form of 'tit for tat' following the War of Independence. The overwhelming majority of cases claiming entitlement to land in Israel, comprise the simple assertion than an ancestor occupied a small piece of land in an area which had been referred to as Palestine and which once formed part of the Ottoman Empire. The assertion may even be backed up by a key which is alleged to have been the front door of a property on the land in question. However, title to the land did not vest in the occupier but another individual who often held it in accordance with the Ottoman land system at the time. This, in reality meant that he held it, directly or indirectly, on behalf of the Ottoman Empire. In simplistic terms, at its highest, in the overwhelming majority of cases the ancestor may have rented a very small parcel of land from, indirectly, the Ottoman Empire. The descendant of that ancestor now claims ownership, as of right, to that land.

No legal system in the world has ever upheld a claim to ownership of land as of right under the circumstances as outlined above. Yet that is the basis of the claim by those who wish to be referred to as Palestinians and the basis of the allegation that 'their' land was 'stolen' from them.

There is a separate argument which is put forward which refers to the right of self-determination. The argument is put in a manner similar to the following. We are Palestinians. We are of the Islamic faith. We do not wish to be governed by Israelis or those of the Jewish faith. Further, as will be seen[2] we do not want to be governed by those of the Islamic faith unless it is within our own state. We wish to govern ourselves in our own land. There would not appear to be anything wrong with this argument except, of course, while one can properly claim self-determination in relation to their own land you cannot so claim it in relation to land which does not belong to you. This brings one to the question: who owns the land presently occupied by Israel?

There are three approaches to this. The first is the biblical approach whereby there is a mass of evidence clearly showing Jewish occupation of an area of land referred to as Israel well before the time of the Muslim invasion in or around 636CE[3] and of course even further than that, well before the advent of Christianity. Equally, after 636CE there is a mass of evidence showing the majority Muslim occupation from then until 1948. However, it has to be emphasized that it is 'an area of land' and it certainly does not follow that it was the same area of land prior to 636CE then as occupied by Israel today. Indeed, the evidence tends to show that it was very substantially less.

The second approach refers to the United Nations vote in 1947, which in turn leads to the legal position resulting from such a vote. This was a result of the situation at that time. The British, held a mandate of the area referred to then as Palestine following the breakup of the Ottoman Empire after the First World War. The British, having been unable to resolve the multiplicity of issues which arose at that time, then returned the land to the United Nations to dispose of it according to the will of the United Nations. The United Nations favoured partition in order to bring what it considered to be a just solution to the problem. The 'Palestinians', supported by their Arab and other Muslim brethren in the Middle East, were against any sovereign state governed by those of the Jewish faith. The Jewish people, while far from satisfied with the

---

[2] P. 30. Jordan.
[3] See p. 14 of the main work.

area of land proposed, agreed to partition in order to have at least some 'home of their own'.[4]

The third approach relates to what happened after the 'Palestinians' and a number of what have been referred to as 'Arab nations' rejected the democratic decision of the United Nation. This, coupled with the second approach above, is at the heart of the present day conflict and clearly identifies where the moral high ground is and where the interests of justice clearly lie. A number of Arab armies declared war on the minority of the Jewish people who occupied the land. This war was, on any view, an aggressive war and as such amounted to a crime against peace and in one sense could equally be argued as being a war crime.[5] The Arab armies lost the war and Israel declared its independence on 14th. May 1948.

It is difficult to moderate one's language. Numerous Arab states waged an aggressive war, having rejected a lawful democratic vote by the United Nations. Yet those nations who voted for partition did not send a single soldier to assist the embryonic state of Israel in its defence of the land that the United Nations had voted should be theirs. Very few nations who voted in support of partition would offer any assistance of any kind whatsoever to the embryonic state. Notwithstanding the overwhelming evidence of an internationally recognised crime against peace[6] for which there is clear legal precedent, not merely political 'opinions', not a single state or individual who took part in the aggressive wars has been called upon to account for their criminality. A criminality which exists up to the present day. One would be hard-pressed even to find a media outlet in the Western world which advocated the prosecution for these crimes against peace or war crimes perpetrated against the Jewish defenders of homeland recognized as theirs by the United Nations vote. Whatever the readers' political views or ideology may be, these clear facts beg the question: what type of world is it when crimes against peace or war crimes arise following the waging of a clearly established aggressive war, yet no action is taken by the international community?

---

[4] Ibid.pp.27-48
[5] Ibid.p.48.
[6] Nuremberg War Crimes Tribunal

It is extremely difficult to understand the purpose of a United Nations body if it does not have the will to enforce its own rules. It is true this was a period close to the end of Second World War were those in positions of power, perhaps understandably, may not have had the stomach for yet further fighting. However, when numerous innocent lives are lost because the United Nations does not wish to enforce its own rules this, in the modern era, quite literally beggars belief and illustrates the hypocrisy of a leading international organ. The unfortunate fact remains that action then may well have prevented many of the issues which exist today, not to mention the saving of numerous lives.

Following Israel's Declaration of Independence, a further legal issue arose and which has not been resolved to this present day. It involved not merely the right of self-determination but whether land could, lawfully, be acquired by conquest. The position in international law prior to January 1918 was that land could be acquired by conquest. Indeed that is how Empires, including the Ottoman, Roman, British and other empires were created. No-one could properly argue that such was illegal. If they did so argue it would not have been upheld by the international community. In January 1918 there were two relevant speeches. The first was on the 5th January 1918 by the British Prime Minister Lloyd George[7]. The second was on the 8th January 1918 by the United States President, Woodrow Wilson, when he stated:

'The day of conquest and aggrandizement is gone by'[8].

On the 11th February 1918, Woodrow Wilson in his famous speech laid down guiding principles to be followed in a nation's approach to peace treaties. In particular he stated:

'There shall be no annexations, no contributions, no punitive damages. Peoples are not to be handed about from one sovereignty to another by an international conference or an understanding between rivals and antagonists. National aspirations must be respected: peoples may now be dominated and governed only by their own consent'.[9] Further, Woodrow Wilson was to emphasize a number of important principles. In particular: 'that peoples and provinces are not to be bartered about from sovereignty to

---

[7] David Lloyd George, *War Memoirs* (London: Ivor Nicholson and Watson, 1933-6), v. 2515-27

[8] Temperley (ed.), *A History of the Peace Conference of Paris,* i. 431-3

[9] Ibid. i. 437

sovereignty as if they were mere chattels and pawns in a game, even the great game, now for ever discredited, of the Balance of Power; but that ….. every territorial settlement involved in this war must be made in the interest and for the benefit of the populations concerned, and not as part of any mere adjustment or compromise of claims amongst rival states…'[10] [11].

At that time period, when it was resolved that no country could obtain land by conquest the one area of land whose ownership was still in a state of 'flux' was that area referred to as Palestine. The suggestion that this is some form of 'game' like 'musical chairs' by somehow suggesting that any acquisition of land by a sovereign power by force after that date is somehow automatically illegal, irrespective of the particular circumstances, and means that in such circumstances the acquisition can only be acquisition as an 'occupier' is little more than 'nonsense upon stilts'. In the case of Israel, issues relating to land were still outstanding in 1918, 1947 and remain to this day. Yet there appears to be an insistence by many that any land Israel occupies after 1948, other than that land which the United Nations voted for, as a result of defending itself from aggressive wars, is somehow occupation as a military occupier. Many European nations feel it is necessary to travel down that route during the present time. They appear to refuse to take into account the crimes against peace and war crimes committed which resulted in the War of Independence. They refuse to take into account the numerous innocent lives lost by those who were doing little more while fighting the War of Independence, than trying to put into practice the vote of the United Nations.

There is yet another important point made by many who, perfectly understandably, answer those who advance the principles of self-determination for the Palestinians under all circumstances which is simply this. Consider: If after the Second World War, the people of Germany had not merely accepted defeat and tried to make the best of their lives for the future but had stated words to the effect: "We support our Fuhrer. He may be dead but his ideology lives on. We will never accept occupation. We do not

---

[10] Ibid. p.439.

[11] An excellent account of the demise of the Right of Conquest is to be found in Sharon Korman's superb work: *The Right of Conquest,* (Clarendon Press Oxford)

accept defeat. We will strive to find a replacement Fuhrer with the same ideology as Hitler and when we do we will come and obtain our revenge against all etc." Are such people nonetheless entitled to the benefit of the doctrine of self-determination? Where is the rule of International Law which permits the people who have waged an aggressive war to automatically, irrespective of the circumstances, remain in a similar position in relation to land than before they waged such a war, when they maintain the same views and ideology which led them to wage an aggressive war in the first place! The Wilsonian principles were the way forward to prevent land being acquired by conquest for the purpose of Empire building. They were never designed to be abused and to be utilised as a sword in order to wage aggressive wars and to continue waging aggressive wars against one's neighbour.

Moving on from the War of Independence and some of its present day consequences, the reader should be aware that following that war, Jerusalem and the area of land known as the Golan Heights did not form part of the State of Israel. In so far as the United Nations vote on partition was concerned, Jerusalem was to be administered under the auspices of a form of International control.

1967 – The Six Day War[12]

In 1967 the Arab armies, led by Abdul Nasser, declared war on the sovereign state of Israel. Not being satisfied by waging an aggressive war in 1948, they were to wage yet another aggressive war. Yet again, these armies committed crimes against peace against the people of the State of Israel. Yet again, no country forming part of the United Nations came to Israel's aid by sending troops to assist in repelling the aggressors. As a result of this war Israel took control of Jerusalem and the Golan Heights which had been used to attack Israel's villages. Numerous, totally innocent people, died as a result of these violent wars of aggression waged by the Arab and Muslim armies against the Jewish people. The suggestion, it is necessary to repeat, that there is a rule of international law whereby when a country wages an aggressive war against another sovereign state and commits crimes against

---

[12] Main work. Pp.58-61

peace or war crimes, if the defending State is victorious it somehow cannot obtain title to land obtained during its defence and protection, but must always remain a military occupier, irrespective of the circumstances, is frankly absurd. Consider this: A state has to conscript its young men and women in order to defend itself and its citizens. A young man dies defending his country from an aggressive attack. His country is, however, winning the war and successfully defending its citizens. The international community places substantial pressure upon the victorious defending state to refrain from further hostilities in order to prevent further loss of life. The defending state succumbs to such pressure, but occupies certain areas of land to minimise the risk of further loss of life from that area of land. The aggressor makes it clear that not only does it not wish to make peace but doesn't even recognize the defending state's right to exist. Unsurprisingly, some years later a further war is waged. This time the defending state's soldiers included the son of the soldier who died in the previous encounter. Again, the defending state is victorious. This time the son dies. Again, the international community bring pressure upon the victorious state to refrain from further hostilities in order to prevent further loss of life. Again, the defending state succumbs to such pressure. The cycle continues resulting in the substantial innocent loss of life to its defending soldiers. This scenario is again quite frankly absurd and the international community by, focusing only on the humanitarian consequences of war, failing to recognize where truth and justice properly lie, ought to be thoroughly ashamed of themselves. In the example provided above one can readily see how a family can be deprived of the lives of a father, a son, a grandson etc. The guilt for such a situation lies not only in the hands of those who took part in the aggressive war to begin with but also institutions such as the United Nations who stood by and did little or nothing to prevent it. Recognizing where law and justice lay and defending it would have prevented or substantially mitigated the carnage which followed and which in one sense continues to apply even today.

The Yom Kippur (Day of Atonement) War[13]

In 1973, some six years after the 'Six day War' the armies of Syria, Egypt and Jordan joined forces in order to wage yet another aggressive war against the sovereign state of Israel. In so far as the international community was concerned the picture was similar to the previous wars. Yet again, not a single nation offered its forces to assist Israel against trying to repel the aggression from its neighbours. The crimes against peace committed by these armies remain, yet again, outstanding without any form of enforcement to the present day. The innocent lives lost by the forces of Israel in repelling the aggression from the invading armies remain totally unrequited through any legal process. It would appear that these states which invaded Israel and waged war against it are somehow immune from prosecution by the various forces of law and order set up by a number of nations in order to punish those who wage aggressive wars on another sovereign state.

Operation Pillar of Defence

On the 10th November 2012 an anti-tank missile fired from Gaza struck an IDF jeep seriously wounding four soldiers. Between the 10th and 13th November 2012 a total of some 206 rockets were fired from Gaza into Israel.[14] Israel responded with numerous airstrikes against Hamas targets, including underground rocket launchers and an ammunition warehouse stocking Iranian made long-range Fajr-5 missiles.

This latest war was to last between 14th and 21st November 2012. During that period hundreds of rockets were fired from Gaza towards the Israeli cities of Beersheba, Ashdod, Ofakim, Tel Aviv and others. Many were intercepted by the Iron Dome missile defence system.

On the 21st November there was an explosion on a bus in Tel Aviv wounding at least 28 people.

---

[13] Ibid. P.61.

[14] Israeli Ministry of Foreign Affairs
http://www.mfa.gov.il/MFA/Terrorism-+Obstacle+to+Peace/Hamas+war+against+Israel/Palestinian_ceasefire_vi
olations_since_end_Operation_Cast_Lead.htm

At 21.00 on the 21st November following substantial diplomatic efforts principally by Egypt and the USA a truce was agreed between Israel and Hamas.

Six Israelis died and 278 were injured. 177 Gazans died and 1,000 were injured. [15]

Operation Protective Edge

In the summer of 2014 Israel mounted a military operation into Gaza. This followed numerous rocket attacks into Israel from Gaza as well as incursions into Israel's sovereign territory. Hamas had created at vast expense numerous tunnels from Gaza into Israeli territory. Their purpose was to enable them to deploy their 'fighters' into Israel in order to carry out terrorist activities in Israel proper and attack Israeli citizens. Destruction of the tunnel system and destruction of the various rocket launching sites were principal aims of Israel's defence forces. According to various sources[16] some 4,564 rockets and mortars had been fired from Gaza into Israel and 34 known tunnel systems were destroyed along with a significant proportion of the Hamas armament store. The fighting lasted some 50 days. At the end some 2,251 Palestinians were killed. 11,231 were injured. 73 Israelis were killed and 1,600 were injured.[17]

In essence, all these wars waged by the Palestinians with or without the support of other armies involved two core claims. The first, that the land of Israel belongs, not to Israelis, but to the Palestinians and secondly, their claim to the right of self-determination within such land.

The absurdity of a literal interpretation to the rule of self-determination and its application, irrespective of the circumstances, has been touched upon above in relation to the position with Germany at the end of the Second World War. Applying that analogy to the present Israel/Palestinian scenario, consider this: The suggestion is that a group of people supported by sovereign states can commit crimes against peace or war crimes, cause the deaths of numerous victims, and yet when it loses its war neither it nor those who supported and instigated the

---

[15] UNHRC
[16] UN
[17] UN OCHA Posted on 23rd June 2015.

aggressive wars are prosecuted. If that were not sufficient, the aggressors seek to argue that they should be 'rewarded' by being able to obtain the land of the sovereign state which was forced to defend itself, with impunity. The victorious state should then be forced to give up its land to the aggressor. In default of such demands that, in the eyes of the aggressor, is justification for waging yet another war in the future. Although the nonsense and lack of merit in the aggressor's argument is self-evident for some reason the wars are often dealt with by many politicians and the media as a 'continuing cycle of violence'. This is true, yet it is not entirely accurate unless it is balanced by the continuing inertia of such organizations as the United Nations who appear content to stand by and let the cycle continue without defending the real victim of the aggressive violence. This, quite frankly is yet but another example which beggars belief.

Do those who die in defence of their own sovereign state do so for nothing? Is the victorious state entitled to nothing for the loss of life of its innocent citizens in defence of their country? What nonsense is this!

The above deals with principal wars. There have been many other wars and skirmishes particularly with Lebanon and Gaza. The story is always the same. Israel is attacked and in consequence is forced to defend itself. It receives no assistance in the form of any offer of the armed forces of other nations from the world's powers to help it in repelling the aggressors. It receives assistance, principally from the USA, particularly in relation to the supply of weaponry in order to defend itself.

The Approach of the Media

What then of the world's media? What does the world's press say following the numerous acts of aggression committed against the sovereign state of Israel? A state which is small in size compared to the land of many of its predatory aggressors? The media possess numerous freedoms in many of the world's civilised countries in order that they are not fettered in bringing to the public's attention grave injustices which have been perpetrated. There are few graver injustices than those caused by mobs of people, often supported by one or more states, which wages not one aggressive war against another sovereign state but a number. What do those guardians of freedoms and liberties say about this appalling criminal behaviour against the sovereign state of Israel?

The approach of many organizations, including the media, again is, quite frankly, unbelievable in the modern era. An era of the rule of law where people have rights, liberties and – it ought not to be forgotten – responsibilities. The broadcasts and reports in relation to violence in the Gaza Strip can be utilised to illustrate the approach of the media generally to the Israel/Palestinian issue. Rarely does the media focus upon the reasons for the wars and various related forms of violence. It is nearly always the same. How many 'Palestinian' civilians were killed? Hardly ever is there a mention of the fact that, when dealing with the violence which so regularly engulfs Gaza, the overwhelming majority of these 'civilians' voted for a terrorist organization to govern them, knowing full well that such organizations seeks the destruction of their neighbour, the sovereign state of Israel. The next step for the media appears to be to subdivide the dead into women and children. Often this is to paint the picture that Israel is the aggressor killing 'innocent women and children'. Rarely is the simple fact mentioned that in war often it is those who are totally innocent who suffer tragic injuries and death, irrespective of any exercise of restraint of an army called upon to defend its people. Rarely is there any detailed mention as to how, for example, in Gaza, Hamas uses the innocent as human shields and appears to care little about using 'civilian' premises from where to fire its rockets. The approach of so many media organizations is the same or similar in every conflict between Israel and the Palestinians.

As an aside, when dealing with Gaza it is perhaps interesting to note that prior to 1948 and the War of Independence the people who occupied Gaza could properly be referred to as Gazans, albeit that Gaza formed part of an area which was referred to as Palestine. The population substantially increased following the War of Independence with many fleeing their homes in Palestine and going to Gaza. Historically, land which included modern-day Gaza was referred to as The Land of the Philistines.[18]

Anybody genuinely interested in the manner in which the Western media report matters concerning Israel when it is locked in conflict with those who seek to destroy it can easily and readily

---

[18] Map. Johnson and Ward c.1863.

research the various and numerous reports over some fifty years or so, even ignoring the War of Independence.

The essential facts contained in the above few paragraphs will have been developed into, on occasions, voluminous pages by the media. The overwhelming majority of which are rarely concerned with accurate news reporting but create propaganda. This propaganda fuels hatred by many against the sovereign state of Israel and does absolutely nothing to resolve the crisis or even discuss the true cause. This hatred does not simply stop at Israel or the Israeli people, but the contamination by this propaganda attaches to Jewish people the world over. This propaganda can properly be described as the propaganda of evil. It spawns boycotts and similar antagonism. The ordinary individual will be confronted with a very similar picture of antagonism, propaganda and prejudice intermittently, throughout the whole period, going back in time since the United Nations vote in 1947 in relation to the partition of Palestine. It is perhaps no wonder that a number of organizations have been set up whose principal aim appears to be simply one of honest and accurate reporting.[19] The fact that any media organization in the 21st century feels driven into doing such a thing such as failing to clearly identify facts and causes, failing to deal fairly with a sovereign state under attack by aggressors, is one of the saddest indictments of those segments of the media in the present modern era.

However it is 'dressed up', if you attack your neighbour who is legally in occupation of his land with the intention of killing him or of doing other forms of harm to him you ought not to be entitled to any sympathy whatsoever, other than from a simple humanitarian perspective if that neighbour successfully defends itself. That perspective ought to be restricted to the truly innocent, particularly the children. Those responsible for the creation of the most appalling propaganda against a state doing its best to defend its citizens ought to realise that had it not been for millions of brave men and women during two World Wars being prepared to defend others against those who wage aggressive attacks, then it is most unlikely that any of the individuals responsible, directly or indirectly, for the creation of the propaganda would be in the position they are today. The media may state that it is they and

---

[19] E.g. 'Honest Reporting'.

they alone who are somehow responsible for creating the doctrine 'freedom of the press/media'. Such a statement would be erroneous. Upholding that cherished doctrine have been numerous people over centuries, including lawyers, politicians and the like who have tried to defend it against all comers. It should not be abused as it appears to be on a regular basis as far as Israel is concerned.   A modern-day picture, reasonably and properly representative of the overall approach of the media can be found in the events which took place in May 2018 involving the Gaza Strip and referred to by those in the Strip as the March of Return.

PART TWO

2018 Gaza riots and the Continuing Development of the Propaganda of Evil

The March of Return

The reader will, hopefully, be aware that the Palestinians principally occupy two areas of land referred to as the 'occupied territories' along the border with Israel. One of those is referred to as the West Bank. The other is known as the Gaza Strip.[20] The Gaza Strip is politically governed by a group known as Hamas which many nations of the civilised world consider to be a terrorist organization. Its ideology is clear. They refuse to recognize the state of Israel and seek its destruction.[21] In the past they have been responsible for infiltrating the land of Israel in many ways, particularly by building 'underground' tunnels and attacking innocent Israeli citizens and Israel's soldiers. There is masses of independent evidence probative of such basic facts.

In May 2018 the terrorist group Hamas urged their supporters to storm the border between Israel and Gaza Strip. According to estimates there were some 40,000 people who had gathered at the border between Israel and Gaza intent on gaining entry into the sovereign state of Israel. The demonstration leading to the attempted forced entry on to the land was organized under the heading: 'March of Return'. There can be little doubt that this was to be a forcible return onto land which the terrorist group Hamas claimed was theirs. On the other side of the fence and guarding the state of Israel were the soldiers of the Israeli Defence force. Wire cutters were used to breach the fence with access into Israel territory. Stones, Molotov cocktails and blazing 'kites' were thrown, which resulted in very substantial damage to acres of land within Israel. The soldiers responded at times with live fire. Many of those taking part in the riots were injured and some tragically lost their lives. The exact numbers are unclear but a reasonable

---

[20] See Main work
[21] Ibid. P. 67.

approximation from the various UN and media reports appear to show Palestinian casualties of approximately 40 dead and some 6,000 injured. The violence in one form or another continued for weeks afterwards. Those individuals who died in support of Hamas and the riots were treated as martyrs, not only by Hamas but by many of the Islamic faith. Further, many governments where Islam was the principal religion supported the Gaza Palestinians and referred, with apparent support, to the martyrdom of those killed during the infiltration and attempted infiltration into the land of the sovereign state of Israel.

The International Response

Most of the international response can succinctly be summed up as being one of outrage. But the outrage was not directed against the terrorist organization or its supporters who attempted by force to unlawfully enter their neighbour's land, throw 'Molotov cocktails', fire sling shots at Israel's defenders as well as burning the crops of their neighbours by the use of burning kites. It was directed against those defending the state. One of the few exceptions being the USA, who firmly lay the blame at Hamas. It is important to examine this response in some detail by looking at the quotations of those in positions of power on the world stage. For, by examining such detail, the reader will get a clearer picture as to how facts can be manipulated to create the evil of propaganda and the prejudice which the state of Israel has regularly suffered. Such examination provides compelling evidence of the underlying themes so regularly put forward, not only in this Annex, but in the main volume itself. It would be useful to begin with the death of a 15 year old boy, by the name of Ayyoub, during the riot and storming of the border fence.

Nickolay Mladenov, UN Special Co-Ordinary for the Middle East Peace Process, on condemning Ayyoub's death called for an investigation into the incident.

He stated: "It is outrageous to shoot at children!" 'Posted on Twitter'[22] "How does the killing of a child in Gaza today help peace? It doesn't! It fuels anger and breeds more killing. Children

---

[22] Jerusalem Post 22nd April 2018.

must be protected from violence, not exposed to it, not killed! This tragic incident must be investigated."

A statement released by the European Union stated: "…full investigation is needed to understand what happened and why. As we once again mourn the loss of lives, the EU calls on the Israel Defence Forces to refrain from using lethal force against unarmed protesters. The priority now must be to avoid any further escalation of violence and loss of life."

Israel's Defence Minister stated: "The only culprits in the death of the 15 year old boy in Gaza are Hamas leaders. Those cowardly leaders hide behind women and children and send them forward as human shields so they can continue to dig tunnels and carry out acts of terrorism against the State of Israel. I repeat to the residents of Gaza: 'To prolong your life, do not go near the fence'."

Observation

It is a tragedy when anyone is killed whether he be 15 or 50. However, it is doubtful whether one needs an enquiry to establish what has occurred for it is a matter of common sense. If thousands of people riot and storm the border of any sovereign nation that sovereign nation will use its forces and rightly so, to defend its land and its people from such attacks. That is its right. It is difficult to moderate one's language when dealing with the statement of Mladenov. It is not a statement made by an ordinary Gazan civilian incensed at what has occurred or even by a newspaper reporter it is a statement made by the Special Co-ordinator for the UN. Let there be no doubt it is little short of a disgrace, which is the appropriate word, when someone who can be presumed to have knowledge of the relevant factual events, who is in a position of power within an organization with the high-sounding name as the 'UN' makes such statements. He must surely know that such a statement will be 'picked up' by those who are anti-Israel, not to mention those who are anti-Semitic, who will use it to further their own particular cause and their own particular ideology. *It is outrageous to shoot at children'.* If a 15 year old boy is part of a group responsible for rioting and storming the border of a sovereign nation then it is reasonably probable that he will be injured and could even die from such injuries. Such is the reality of life when you are part of a mob which storms your neighbour's border. This is aggravated further when you appear to be part of a mob which supports an ideology which denies your neighbour's right to exist and you are intent on killing them. If that were not sufficient the EU's statement, if accurately reported, erroneously states that the protesters were 'unarmed'. Those responsible for issuing such a statement must, as with the UN, be aware of the true facts, or at the very least ought to be aware of such facts. They must know that what is being said is likely to be reported worldwide and must surely realise the consequences of such reporting in the minds of ordinary individuals. True, it is the protesters may not have been armed as soldiers are, yet they were not 'unarmed'. Knives, stones, slings, Molotov cocktails, burning kites and the like are all forms of arms. They were a violent mob, tens of thousands strong, intent on causing as much damage as possible to Israel and its soldiers. Why wasn't that clearly stated?

The response of a Human Rights Group

The 'so-called' human rights group, Amnesty International, described the response of the forces defending Israel and its people as 'deplorable'. Philip Luther, on behalf of the group, stated:

"This is another horrific example of the Israeli military using excessive force and live ammunition in a totally deplorable way… This is a violation of international standards, in some instances committing what appear to be wilful killings constituting war crimes".[23]

Observation

The reason that the words 'so-called' are used is simply because one would reasonably expect that any human rights group, properly so-called, would recognize that Israel, its forces and its people also have human rights in exactly the same way as everyone else. There was no 'violation of international standards'; no 'wilful killings' and no 'war crimes'. It was a sovereign state acting in a perfectly lawful manner in defence of itself and its citizens.[24] Just because you call yourself a 'human rights' group

---

[23] Jerusalem Post 15th May 2018.
[24] See below. Part Three- Self-Defence.

does not necessarily mean that you truly understand the meaning of human rights. Human rights are not the exclusive province of Palestinians or those who are employed by Amnesty International. Yet no proper attempt appears to have been made to recognize this and to bring this factor to bear when considering the various issues. Had they made such an attempt, a proper picture, or at least a more accurate one, could be created for those who listened to or read such statements. Unfortunately however, this group appears unable or unwilling to attempt such a balancing exercise or, so it would appear generally, any form of reasonable balancing exercise as far as the sovereign state of Israel is concerned. To take a hypothetical example: If the offices of Amnesty International, or any alleged human rights group for that matter, was attacked by a violent mob intent on doing the occupants harm or worse and when the police arrived this mob carried on, threatening the police with various weaponry including knives, is it really being suggested that if, after giving the appropriate warnings, the police used their weapons to protect the occupants of the offices, could they, justifiably, be criticised by anyone? Is there anything wrong with that? Let us assume that the mob was not say, ten or twenty strong, but were numbered in their thousands. During the defence by the police of the offices some of the mob died as a result of their injuries. Would the police be accused of 'war crimes'?

Turkey's response

The President Erdogan of Turkey strongly condemned the Israeli government over its 'inhuman attack' on Palestinians. In a speech broadcast by Turkish state Television to Turkish students in London, President Erdogan described Israel as 'a terrorist state' and had committed 'genocide' against the Palestinian people.[25]

Observation

For those genuinely interested in Turkish politics it may be useful to peruse what was occurring in Turkish politics around that time and for a significant period previously. It will be apparent that Erdogan had been seeking more and more power for himself and

---

[25] Reported by the Times of Israel, by Alexander Fulbright 14/5/18.

his position is fairly close to being akin to that of a dictator. When the President of a sovereign state uses the kind of language he used against not only one of his neighbours but a state which, on any view, has a political and legal system substantially superior to his own in its ability to deliver democracy, fairness and justice it ought to be unnecessary to add anything further.

The twenty-eighth regular session of the Human Rights Council

A resolution for the purpose of dispatching an Independent, International Commission of Inquiry to Investigate Human Rights Violations in the Context of Large – Scale Civilian Protests in the Occupied Palestinian Territory was debated in May 2018. The resolution was adopted by a vote of 29 in favour, 14 abstentions and two against. The draft text of the resolution was introduced by Pakistan on behalf of the organization of Islamic Cooperation. This organization was formed in 1969. It has 57 member states, 56 of which are also members of the UN. The majority religion in the overwhelming majority of the states (all save four) who voted for the resolution appears to be either Islam or Roman Catholic. The two countries who voted against the resolution were the United States of America and Australia. Two countries who pride themselves on the importance of secularism within their respective states and where the practice of religion is a true human right, as opposed to a particular religion specifically favoured by the state and those in power within the state. To what extent religious prejudices and bigotry played its part is of course unclear. However, it is self-evident that none of the states had a 'Jewish' majority there being of course only one state in the world with such a majority. That sentence in itself is telling to any reasonably fair-minded person.

A number of nations spoke during the discussion. In essence what was stated included the following:[26]

'The Council condemned the disproportionate and indiscriminate use of force by the Israeli occupying forces against Palestinian civilians, including in the context of peaceful protests, particularly in the Gaza Strip'.

---

[26] OHCHR I Human Rights Council

Luxembourg considered *'that the violence carried out recently by Israeli forces was unacceptable. This was excessive use of force and in breach of international humanitarian law'*.

Argentina observed that *'the escalation of* (the acts of violence) *which had led to a tragedy not just for the Palestinian people, but for humankind. The excessive and disproportionate use of force was in violation of international human rights'*.

It further called for a *sovereign state for Palestinians within the pre-1967* borders.

Guinea firmly condemned the acts carried out by the occupying force of Israel. *'The only crime of the Palestinian people was their wish to live a life in dignity and freedom'*.

Albania expressed the view that *'the right to protest peacefully was a fundamental human right to be respected by all'*.

Niger *firmly condemned the use of excessive force by Israel against peaceful protesters in the Gaza Strip, who had been protesting the transfer of the United States Embassy to Jerusalem...'*

Djibouti *recognized and supported the right of Palestinians to self-determination and regretted the recent events that had undermined prospects for peace. Israel's disregard for international resolutions had led to the explosion of violence in the Gaza Strip. Djibouti asked Israel to respect its international obligations, to end the blockade of Gaza and to cease its settler policy'*.

Independent Commission for Human Rights called upon the Human Rights Council *'to investigate the excessive and disproportionate use of force by the Israeli occupying forces against Palestinian citizens. It requested the Council to look into the grave violations of human rights and international humanitarian law committed by the Israeli occupying forces in Gaza, Potentially amounting to war crimes, these violations were perpetrated against the peaceful Great March of Return...'*

International Commission of Jurists was concerned *'at the many killings and serious injuries associated with the excessive, unjustified or otherwise unlawful use of force by Israel, including the killing of a number of children...'*

International Federation for Human rights Leagues *'strongly condemned the killing and injury of the Palestinians who had been peacefully protesting...'*

In addition to the above there were numerous other organizations many supporting Arab causes generally, with similar observations to the above. Two organizations – United Nations Watch and World Jewish Congress – rejected the various comments condemning Israel.[27]

The nature of the comments referred to above, while specific to the March of Return are comments which tend to undermine the sovereign state of Israel. They are not that dissimilar in nature to those comments uttered against the sovereign state of Israel by various individuals, groups and countries over many years. The analysis which follows clearly demonstrates the unfairness and unjust nature of many such comments when other relevant circumstances are properly included. Many such types of comment have followed after each of the various wars Israel has had to suffer since its creation in the modern era.

It is essential when deciding whether observations and comments are fair and just to examine them carefully. The fact that such comments emanate from individuals, groups or organizations with high-sounding names such as 'Human Rights Council' or 'Ambassador' or the 'State of...' or ' Special Prosecutor' or even the United Nations itself, have little relevance. It is the substance of the comment which has to be examined. The individual who is stating it is not material in relation to deciding the accuracy or fairness of the comment.

However, what is important is that all these organizations know that their comments are likely to be picked up by the media generally and reproduced to a worldwide audience. It follows that if the comments are misleading, false, unfair and unjust then propaganda is likely to have been created. Consider the above comments.

Exposing propaganda and falsehoods

'Peaceful Protests'

If thousands of people supporting a terrorist organization charge the border of a sovereign state using sling shots, bricks, Molotov cocktails and firebombing the agricultural land of the sovereign

---

[27] OHCHR I Human Rights Council 21/5/2018 p. 3/9

state with kites it is not a peaceful protest by any stretch of the imagination.

'The only crime of the 'Palestinians' was their wish to live a life in dignity and freedom'

The majority in Gaza voted for a terrorist organization whose principal objective, by their own admission, was to destroy the lives of its neighbouring people. This is inconsistent with wanting to live a peaceful life in dignity and freedom. The government which these people supported used vast amounts of money to build tunnels and acquire arms in support of their violent aims. They teach their children to hate their neighbour, hate Israel and hate all Jewish people. They falsely and wrongly accuse their neighbour of stealing 'their' land in order that they may obtain land which never did (except in a few very rare instances) belong to them or to any of their forefathers.[28] They use the falsehoods and propaganda in an attempt to justify the obtaining of a state for themselves. Whether they ought to have a state for themselves is a wholly different question than the attempt to justify the obtaining of such a state based upon such falsehoods. These actions are hardly those of a people who wish to live their life in dignity and freedom!

'....a sovereign state within the pre-1967 borders'

These are people who wage war, or support the waging of war against its neighbour,[29] killing and maiming innocent Israeli men women and children. When they lose that war they then suggest that somehow one ought to forget about the crimes against peace in the waging of that war. Tell that to the families of the innocent soldier who lost his life while doing nothing but defending his state and his fellow countrymen against unlawful attacks. Further, if that is not sufficient, they suggest that not only should the world forget about the crimes against peace and war crimes that had been committed, inherent in the waging of such aggressive war but go on to argue that the victims of the aggressive behaviour should return to the borders before the aggressive war was waged. The

---

[28] The land at the relevant periods since Roman times belonged to the Ottoman Empire, thereafter to the League of Nations. See main volume
[29] 1967 6 Day War see p. 59.

innocent lives that the aggressors took are they to be valueless? Tossed to one side to appease the politicians? What nonsense is this?

'...to end the blockade of Gaza.'

When Hamas incites its people to wage yet another war against the sovereign state of Israel and its people, it needs armaments and materials for building its tunnels. Without relevant control such armaments can readily be brought in via the Mediterranean Sea. This is self-evident by simply looking at a map of the area. These armaments, almost certainly, could include highly sophisticated weaponry including missiles with advanced guidance systems and the like, to be used against the towns and cities of the sovereign state of Israel. This weaponry would be supplied by other nation states using organizations such as Hamas and others as some form of proxy to further their own interests within the area. How ridiculous it is to suggest that the blockade should be ended and then by compelling inference the destructive weaponry could enter without any impediment.

USA withdraws from participation in the United Nations Human Rights Council

On the 20th June 2018, perhaps arguably the most powerful nation in the world announced that it was withdrawing from the United Nations Human Rights Council. Speaking with US Ambassador Nikki Haley, Secretary of State Mike Pompeo said the UN had "become an exercise in shameless hypocrisy, with some of the world's worst human rights abuses going ignored."

Ambassador Haley, an excellent American ambassador, had previously stated that the US would only remain in the body if "essential reforms were achieved." She made it clear that adequate reforms had not been achieved. She further stated: the decision was an affirmation of US respect for Human Rights, a commitment that "does not allow us to remain a part of a hypocritical and self-serving organization that makes a mockery of human rights." Further, "disproportionate focus and unending hostility toward Israel, is clear proof that the council is motivated by political bias, not by human rights." The 'chronic bias' against Israel had been a regular complaint by the US of the UNHRC. Other states either criticised the US decision or regretted it. Thus the UK's Foreign Secretary Boris Johnson said: "The United States' decision to withdraw from the Human Rights Council is regrettable… We've made no secret of the fact that the UK wants to see reform of the Human Rights Council, but we are committed to working to strengthen the council from within…"

The problem with the UK's approach and those of other nations who 'regretted' the decision, albeit that the approach at first sight may appear to be diplomatically understandable, lies in two questions: Firstly, how long are you prepared to wait before accepting that adequate reforms from within are either nor going to happen or are unlikely to happen? Secondly, the reason for the withdrawal is not simply about the lack of credibility of the Council in relation to human rights but on basic issues of fairness to another sovereign state. It is little short of appalling the way this organization has treated the sovereign state of Israel over many years. Thus the endemic bias against the sovereign state of Israel by the UNHRC is not merely inherent but has become so obvious to the overwhelming majority of people who take a real interest and balanced approach to affairs in the Middle East concerning Israel, that it is surprising that the withdrawal by at least one great nation has taken so long. Let there be no doubt, the US is a great nation. It has democratically elected leaders. It has a voting system fairer than many other countries. It has a written constitution. Those features by themselves are a starting point of credibility when human rights are being considered. When it is plainly obvious that other nations are regularly voting for or against a resolution simply by joining together, not so it would appear on the basis of principle or what is right and just, but on the basis of ethnicity or religion then it is unsurprising that another nation or other nations are unlikely to want their own normative standards to be undermined by being associated with such an organization. If a nation state is aware that there are other nation states on the Council who apparently have an inherent hatred towards another sovereign state based upon racial or religious grounds how can such a nation state regularly justify being part of such an organization? In such circumstances how can a nation state justify using the hard-earned money of its taxpayers in support of such an organization?[30]

The type of propaganda which has been created against the state of Israel is not 'normal' propaganda, if such a thing exists. It is the propaganda of evil. This type of propaganda can be properly described as evil for a very simple reason. This is not propaganda which has been created by the odd piece of false news or propaganda which has been created to undermine or which has the effect of undermining an individual or even a few individuals. This is propaganda which has been created, the effect of which is to undermine a whole state and its people. If that isn't sufficient, it has the 'knock-on' effect of undermining Jewish people everywhere because of the association of the religion with the state of Israel. Many people who listening to this type of propaganda, whenever they hear the phrase 'Jewish State', are quick to condemn Israel as being a racist state and some, notably South Africa, attempt to associate this racism with the abhorrent apartheid system which prevailed in that country for so long. However the most basic analysis immediately demonstrates the absurdity of that proposition and how those who actually make that allegation should ask themselves whether it is not they who, in truth, are racist. Consider this: The complaint is that to call Israel a Jewish State is racist. What is the principal religion of say, the United Kingdom; Ireland; Saudi Arabia; France; the Vatican etc.?

---

[30] The author has been advocating a withdrawal from the UNHRC for some time. The reason is not because a decision may have gone against Israel, simply because one does not agree with a decision is not a ground for a withdrawal. It is not 'a' decision which is relevant it is 'numerous' decisions. The inherent bias and prejudice towards the sovereign State of Israel is endemic within the organization. No country should be a party to an organization which so regularly denies fairness and justice to a sovereign State. Many of the countries which remain accept that the organization has a problem in the way it deals with issues concerning Israel which is diplomatic language for recognizing such inherent bias. However, these countries wish to change the organization from within. That is most unlikely to occur unless one is able to change the 'psyche mentality' of many of its members in order that they vote on 'principle' and not 'politics' or automatically giving support for a group simply on the basis of a shared religion or the support of a particular religion. Unfortunately to achieve such an objective would require a 'sea change' in such 'psyche mentality'. This is most unlikely to occur.

All these states have a recognized principal religion which is other than Judaism. No-one would accuse any of them as being 'racist' simply because the nation's state principal religion is Protestant or Islam or Roman Catholic etc. If the Vatican, for example, were to expressly state 'we are a Roman Catholic state' all that they would be doing is stating what to the overwhelming majority of the rest of the world is, 'as plain as a pikestaff', self-evident and obvious.

Whatever the reader's personal ideology or political persuasion one short series of facts are properly undeniable. Over the past seventy years or so the attempts to resolve the 'conflict' between Israel and the Palestinians and to prevent wars regularly breaking out with the consequential loss of life have been literally numerous. They have involved some of the finest politicians of the time from many sovereign nations, including a variety of Prime Ministers. If that were not sufficient it would certainly appear that the majority of right-minded people involved, both Israeli and Palestinian, would also like to see a true peace. Most families – Israeli and Palestinian – wish to bring up their children in an atmosphere of peace, not worrying whether an explosive missile is likely at any moment to fly through the wall of their home. The fact remains that all these attempts by others, whatever the good intentions, have failed. This failure has resulted in the consequential loss of substantial human life at various intervals throughout the last seventy years. The same as all these attempts have failed in the past, as 'night follows day' they will continue to fail in the future unless there is a substantial change in the approach of the various nations involved who are genuinely, trying to bring about a peaceful solution. This is not a situation whereby diplomats can simply try and do some sort of 'deal' involving for example 'money' or a forced 'compromise'. Those who think that it can be done that way have learned nothing from the previous seventy years.

PART THREE

The Doctrine of Self Defence

Its meaning, interpretation and application

It ought to be clear from all the above that a number of those nations and individuals who substantially criticise Israel do so because they consider Israel's response to be a disproportionate one to the riots at its border and the entry and attempted entry to the sovereign state of Israel. The public are entitled to assume that when a civilised nation or organization appoints someone to a position of power enabling them to provide a view on the situation in the conflict between Israel and Palestinians, that that individual would at least know the relevant law. If they are correct in their knowledge of the law then no complaint can properly be made. If they are incorrect in their knowledge then drastic consequences can and do occur. Some of the obvious consequences include quotations from individuals, as above, which are published via the media to an audience of millions, if not billions, of ordinary decent law abiding people worldwide. The view expressed is believed to be correct by the majority of these individuals simply because of the individual who states it. If it is incorrect it lends succour to the anti-Semite, (meaning in this context anti-Jewish); to the individual who is anti-Israel; to the terrorist attempting to get the world to accept his unlawful approach and numerous others.

The media tend to appear to literally 'jump on' anything which undermines the State of Israel without even attempting to explain to its readers, listeners or viewers what the true legal position is. One finishes up with a quasi-Biblical quote such as 'it's an eye for an eyelash'. A quote which the individual who uttered it would no doubt argue was not in any way anti-Semitic (meaning anti-Jewish) or anti-Israel but just happened to relate to 'Old Testament' teachings. Was there nothing in New Testament teachings which could be said to be similarly appropriate without recourse, by inference, to the classic Old Testament phrase? Did he not realise that such a phrase would be reported by the media? Or the vitriolic attack by the modern-day ruler of Turkey whose rule is akin to a dictator or quasi-dictator. Let there be no doubt that it would appear that many of those who have uttered their various comments substantially critical of the methods used by Israel in defending its borders have little or no understanding of what the relevant law relating to self defence is.

Further, they have little or no understanding of the meaning of 'proportionality' in the context of the riots which took place. If that were not sufficient, they also appear to 'bandy about' high-sounding phrases such as 'international humanitarian law', ' fundamental human rights' and the like without properly understanding the meaning of such phrases or indeed even the correct meaning of basic 'human rights' in the context of the Gaza situation. If even that was not sufficient, the various segments of the media also appear to have little interest in correcting the totally misleading picture which has been produced, if not in some cases, manufactured, for its viewers, listeners or readers. It is necessary to explain why the approach taken by most, if not all, of the individuals referred to above as well as others is not merely wrong but obviously and manifestly so. A step by step approach is essential in order to eventually have a clear understanding of the relevant concept of self-defence.

The words used namely, 'self-defence', are words which are known to the vast majority of the world's people. I emphasize 'words'. Their meaning is a totally different matter. That meaning is a mixture of law and fact. It is true that the meaning is somewhat complex but it is not that difficult to understand providing a 'step by step' approach is taken. If that method is not adopted the result is some of the absurd observations referred to above. Whenever Israel is involved and the issue of self-defence arises numerous individuals accuse Israel of a violation of human rights law; war crimes and the like, although it would appear as referred to above that many appear not to properly understand the meaning of those phrases.

Human rights, as a distinct branch of the law, has existed since soon after the conclusion of the Second World War. A useful starting point in a time line would be the Declaration of Human Rights.[31] A declaration which is not recognized by many nations as having legal validity simply because there has been no 'statute' encompassing the specific words contained within the Declaration.

---

[31] Universal Declaration of Human Rights. 10th December 1948.

The European Convention on Human Rights and the Human Rights Act both having legal validity in their respective jurisdictions.

However, prior to the European Convention on Human Rights and prior to the Second World War there was one rule which could properly be stated as being a human right which had existed since time immemorial. That is to say, since the earliest period of time. It is not merely a fundamental rule of Human Rights Law but fundamental to civilisation itself. Yet you will not find it expressly[32] in the European Convention or in the Human Rights Act, for example. So vital is it to civilization that it is doubtful whether any sovereign parliament which believes it has ultimate power to make or unmake any law, would or could lawfully be able to repeal the rule. It is a true rule of Fundamental Law.[33] That rule is the **right** of every human being to use such force as is reasonable[34] in all the circumstances to defend himself, other human beings, his property and his land. That right, when it comes to property and land may be subject to certain responsibilities and statute law, depending upon the political ideology of the state in question. However, the right to defend oneself and other human beings from any unlawful attack is fundamental. When the right is being exercised not by an individual but by a sovereign state on behalf of its citizens, then the relevant responsibility is the doctrine of proportionality. It is sometimes said that the right of self-defence has a different meaning in the international forum to its

---

[32] There is reference to it in Article 2(2) but such reference is in order for it to be utilised to deny the 'Right to Life' as opposed to an existing right on its own.

[33] The UK is one of a number of nations which does not recognize the concept of Fundamental Law as being the most superior law. It further believes that Parliament is free to make or unmake any law it wishes. There are those who have demonstrated how this statement cannot possibly be right. However, that is to detract from the subject matter of this Annex.

[34] In the ECHR Article 2 the word 'absolutely' necessary is used in place of 'reasonably' necessary. However, it is doubtful whether this is any more than semantics for when force is used to quell a riot or insurrection (Article 2(2)(c)) Further, what is 'absolutely' necessary is almost certainly likely to depend on what was 'reasonably' necessary in the prevailing circumstances, For example the numbers, weaponry, motivation and objectives of the rioters.

meaning when the right is exercised by the individual. This suggestion is inherently doubtful and potentially confusing for reasons which are not necessary to delve into here; however proportionality applies both when the right is exercised in the international arena just as it applies to the private individual. It is necessary to emphasize that this doctrine of proportionality is exactly that, a doctrine. It is a term of art. One cannot simply look in a dictionary to find its meaning. The rule of the right of self-defence forms not only the law of all civilized nations but is and always has been an essential rule of International Law. The reason for that statement is simple, for how can any form of International Law be recognized by states in the international arena, if that state does not have a right to defend itself from others waging an aggressive war against it. It may be said that the right of self-defence is not a true right for it only comes into play when there has been a violation of the law by, for example, some form of attack or if death ensues when the expressly stated Human Right to Life has been violated. The difficulty with that argument is that as a matter of common sense the doctrine of self-defence clearly existed before there was any law as we understand it today. That doctrine was a true right exercised by a human being.

The question then arises as to what is 'reasonable force' and what is the meaning of 'proportionality'? Force which is 'disproportionate' by definition is unlikely to be reasonable or absolutely necessary. The question then is what is 'disproportionate'? Before it is possible to answer that question again it is essential to know the law. It is necessary to repeat, you do not look up in a dictionary the meaning of the word 'proportionate' and come to a conclusion. If you do you will add one and one and make three! It is a term of 'legal art'. In order to ascertain its meaning a very helpful contributing legal explanation was provided by the English House of Lords in a leading case[35] The Court properly stated:

"If there has been an attack so that self defence is reasonably necessary, it will be recognized that a person defending himself <u>cannot weigh to a nicety</u> (underlining the author's) the exact measure of defensive action. If the jury thought that that in a moment of unexpected anguish a person

---

[35] Palmer v R 1971 AC 814.

attacked had only done what he honestly and instinctively thought necessary, that would be the most potent evidence that only reasonable defensive action had been taken..."[36]

This classic statement of law has been adopted and applied in numerous countries worldwide. Further, there are highly respected legal authorities whereby one does not have to wait to be attacked before exercising the right of self-defence, which are unnecessary to refer to in this annex.

Applying the law, putting to one side such complexities as the meaning of words such as 'reasonable', 'absolutely', 'proportionate' and the like simply consider the following. A young boy approaches a group of soldiers. He appears unarmed. He is waving a white flag. Is it permissible to shoot the boy using live ammunition? It is suggested that the overwhelming majority of people reading this somewhat extreme example would unhesitating say no. It would be unreasonable because it would amount to disproportionate force in the circumstances. Such force would not be considered 'absolutely necessary'. If the answer is no, what would be the reaction if, say, the previous week another youth had done the same thing and on approaching the soldiers, who had held their fire on seeing that he was only a boy and that he was waving the flag of 'peace' or 'surrender', the youth then detonated a suicide belt and killed one or more of the soldiers? The group that he belonged to hailed him as a martyr, as did many nation states around the world. His family were rewarded with a substantial sum of money. He was held up by a governmental organization as a shining example of what was expected of the citizens. Any soldier who would have shot the boy would have been condemned by many, if not all, of the various individuals referred to above. This simple example and it is possible to provide numerous others which are far more straightforward and much easier to answer, illustrates the difficulties and the necessity for the words of the wise judge referred to above. It is essential to always try and have a clear grasp of the relevant facts and not to get bogged down in the meaning of certain specific legal words, which, as stated, are often terms of art. This essence applies not merely to individuals but to all media outlets involved in publishing and spreading news.

---

[36] Per Lord Morris.

In the present situation relating to the March of Return those who tragically were killed were part of an angry militant mob of not one or two or even a dozen but of tens of thousands. History shows that their government has encouraged and continues to encourage violence against its neighbour resulting in the death, maiming or injury of numerous innocent men women and children over the years. Mothers in a nearby Israeli village have often suffered attacks when rockets hit the walls of their property while getting their children ready for school.[37] It is when defensive violence is used in these kinds of situations that the immortal words of this famous judge referred to above, ring loud and clear.

Why then do these individuals some with the 'high-sounding names' referred to above state what is so obviously false? These individuals know or ought to know the nature of the violence which had taken place and know or ought to know that which they have stated is often false or, at best, misleading (some of the violence could be seen on the television) yet they persist in making such factually false comments. The media know that this was not a 'peaceful protest' yet why do they persist in reporting something which they know or ought to know is false without making such falsity clear? In the alternative, why don't they make it clear that there was a riot at the border with thousands of people attempting to force entry into the sovereign state of Israel, many with sling shots containing stones, 'Molotov' cocktails, burning kites being sent to destroy the fields and crops of their neighbours and the like? Such would surely be more accurate reporting. Is it that by reporting accurately they think they will sell fewer newspapers or that their television audience will be smaller? Is it that their audience will be greater if they show the body of a teenager who they can then describe as a child? Is it the ideological views of those in positions of power within the particular media outlet or of their financial backers which are, to the media outlet, the only views which matter?

It is not, of course, just the media. As has been seen, it is also numerous politicians or civil servants in organizations with the high-sounding names such as the United Nations Human Rights Commission who seek to create a similar injustice to the state of Israel and its people. Truth, fairness, accuracy can all be sacrificed

---

[37] Israeli town of Sderot e.g.

upon the altars of their subjective opinions. This, however, is but a small part of the overall picture of a combination of a 21st century news media; certain politicians and civil servants. Throughout the world there are numerous examples of violence ranging from skirmishes, riots to 'mini' wars. Indeed, at the time of writing[38] 86 people are reported to have died during violent clashes in Nigeria. Thirty-two people have died following attacks in Mali. Yet to find these news items it is necessary to search through the internet or Teletext news services. These news items do not appear to be worthy of inclusion in the 'main news' bulletins or given significant 'column inches' in the newspapers. When however it concerns Israel, a rare democratic nation in the cauldron of the Middle East with a voting system which is arguably much fairer than many in the Western world, the media and some of the politicians who seek it out, appear to consider themselves justified in making attack after attack upon the sovereign state. To simply state that such media outlets and individuals are biased is wholly inadequate and a misuse of language.

Many civilised nations in the world have recognized the importance of prohibiting incitement to racial hatred. Some, at long last, have legislation in place in at least an attempt to deal with the situation.[39] Thus the religious leader who, from the pulpit, advocates violence against another religious group could, in theory at least, be prosecuted. Most people would agree with such legislation. However, it is equally necessary to protect various freedoms enjoyed by those who savour their liberties, such as freedom of speech generally and in particular its inclusion within the 'sound bite' of 'freedom of the press'. The problems occur when freedoms of this nature are abused. Of course one of the most obvious examples of such abuse is when freedom of speech is used to create evil propaganda against the innocent. This can occur when such abusers of the relevant freedom attempt to paint the victim of an attack as somehow the aggressor.

Consider this: The Imam or Ayatollah advocates the destruction of Israel and the killing of Israelis. Because the majority of Israelis are of the Jewish faith it is often a simple process to infer, rightly or wrongly, that the reality is the destruction not merely of the State of Israel but of all those of the Jewish faith. Such an

---

[38] 25th June 2018
[39] E.g. U.K. Racial and Religious Hatred Act 2006.

individual would appear to fall within the clear wording of the statutory prohibition against stirring up racial or religious hatred. Now consider the person who is anti-Israel or anti-Jewish or the individual whose ideology is against the State of Israel and its people. He is in a position of power within a media outlet, either as owner, editor or the like and insists on portraying Israel in the worst possible light. He ensures that false and misleading information is supplied to his audience. In the alternative, If not in itself false and misleading, he attempts to produce a totally false picture. What then is the effect?

What is the effect of pictures of a young Arab boy being held in the arms of his grieving parents having been shot, without any attempt whatsoever to provide the full picture or to explain the circumstances? Or even when there is evidence that the picture is from a wholly different situation in a different place at a different time. For example the issue of the explosive suicide belt as referred to above. The answer is self-evident. Such misleading accounts and pictures 'stir up' hatred against the State of Israel and its people. Indirectly, it stirs up hatred in the minds of many who are against those of the Jewish religion. It enables those who wish to boycott Israel for example in the present so-called BDS movement, to claim a justification for their actions. Yet those responsible for this propaganda claim, or would claim, so-called rights such as 'freedom of the press'. They would say that 'they' did not utter any threatening words; 'they' had no intention to stir up racial hatred; 'they' were merely printing a news story in the 'public interest' for the benefit of their readers and the like. Yet they know or ought to know that because of the way the story has been presented within the newspaper or other media outlet, it was likely to be held up by the terrorists in front of, for example, the youth of Gaza with words to the effect of: 'look the whole world is behind us'; the television images are used to encourage the youth of Gaza and illustrate how the whole world is watching. How 'our day' will soon be here. The propaganda of evil is created just as much as the express words of the Ayotallah or Iman uttered from the pulpit inciting such evil. Freedom of speech does not permit the claimant to use it in order to deploy the propaganda of evil. It ought to be irrelevant whether such deployment occurs through the bigot from the pulpit or whether it is by a so-called 'respectable' newspaper; a nation's diplomat; an employee of any United

Nations organization or the leader of a state. Propaganda of evil is propaganda of evil whether it be direct or indirect and irrespective of the position of the individual who is actually stating the relevant words. The fact that such words create a false and misleading picture with the effect of inciting racial hatred in the minds of those so easily led is one of the most relevant factors.

Quite frankly, there is simply no place in any civilised world or within a combination of civilised nations for the present approach taken by many of these individuals and media outlets. Let there be no doubt this book totally abhors the false and misleading approach of many in relation to the publication of stories concerning the sovereign state of Israel and its fight against terrorist organizations and others who would seek to destroy it. Equally, it totally supports those who use their abilities within the media to create a fair and balanced picture and to publish and deploy the same. Constructive criticism of anyone, which includes a sovereign state, on matters of public interest is to be applauded. Propaganda created from a false and misleading picture is to be condemned.

PART FOUR

The Road to Peace

A necessary step already taken and essential steps which have to be taken

The starting point of any road which could lead to a genuine and lasting peace between two peoples who have been, in reality, at war, in one form or another with each other for some seventy years, requires a clear acceptance of certain essential facts. These are that one does not sacrifice right for wrong or justice for injustice or good for evil in order to obtain some form of temporary respite. It is essential to recognize and state without fear any fact which properly ought to be unarguable without fear or favour. For example, for some reason, politicians are loathe to mention that the overwhelming majority of terrorists throughout the world are of the Islamic faith. It doesn't matter whether they are Hamas, Palestinian supporters of Hamas, Hezbollah, Al-Queda, ISIS, or any one of numerous other groups throughout the world. They are all, or the overwhelming majority, of the Islamic faith and they use this faith to attract their recruits and the like. The faith provides the power in their ability to recruit, not all but numerous members to support their 'cause'. One rarely, if ever in modern times, finds such groups containing the majority of those of the Jewish, Protestant, Catholic, Hindu, Sikh or anyone of the numerous other recognized faiths. These are facts that are known to virtually everyone in the world who takes even a modicum of interest into what is happening in the world and in particular the Middle East. However, that does not mean, and under no circumstances should it be interpreted to mean, that all Muslims are terrorists! There are millions of Muslims around the world in numerous different countries who are ordinary, decent, hardworking, law-abiding people just like those of all the other religions. One must never 'tar an individual with the same brush' as others simply because of their faith. Equally, one must not deny a fact simply because one is concerned that it may not be thought politically correct to mention it. Religion is relevant to so many issues in this conflict apart from some of those referred to above such as the voting arrangements of certain states which form the UNHRC.

For the first time a sign of recognition as to the principal source of the problem came in the form of evidence from the United Nations. The European Parliament in 2018 adopted legislation designed to prevent substantial financial assistance being given to the Palestinian Authority who was using it to teach hatred in educational establishments.[40] The legislation was introduced by the parliament's Committee on Budgetary Control in March 2018 and aimed to ensure that all programmes financed with EU money should 'reflect common values such as freedom, tolerance and non-discrimination within education'. It is clear that billions of dollars have been given by the EU to the Palestinian Authority over a period of some ten years for promoting education and teaching core European values. This money has of course come from the various member states and provided to those states by the hardworking taxpayers of the respective nations. It is equally plain that notwithstanding these vast sums hatred has been taught in schools, in the home and in other places where there has been a form of social gathering. The EU must have been or ought to have been well aware of this for a substantial period of time. It continued to fund and send more and more money, when it knew or ought to have known that such funds were being used in places where the teaching of the hatred of Israelis and hatred of the Jewish people was the norm as opposed to the exception. Did it really think that if the taxpayers of the respective member states were aware of this they would have supported where such money was going? This money, or some of it, was eventually likely to be used, directly or indirectly, to create a terrorist. Someone who would have little or no hesitation in blowing up a train or a bus in a nation state in the West; killing those in the police or armed forces whose jobs involved defending innocent civilians of their state.

It literally beggars belief that an organization such as the European Parliament can provide vast sums of money knowing or when it ought to know, that these sums are being used in the perpetuation of hatred which eventually in many cases can result in the creation of a terrorist, or suicide bomber. An individual or organization who provides money to a terrorist organization directly is likely, in accordance with the law of many nations, to face trial for a very serious criminal offence. If found guilty would rightly be sent to prison for a

---

[40] Reported in the Jerusalem Post on April 20th 2018.

substantial period. Why should the European Parliament be somehow exempt from similar enforcement just because it has the high-sounding name of the 'European Parliament'? Why should those individuals who were party to the obtaining and distribution of such monies be exempt just because of who they are?

In the main work it was made clear that there will never be true peace in the region without proper and adequate education.[41] This is not merely desirable but essential. It has not been done for some seventy years. There has not been any true peace for this time. True peace means exactly that. 'True' peace is a peace accepted by the overwhelming majority of the citizens directly involved. This is the first sign, the first glimmer of hope yet, if it is not pursued with due and proper diligence, there will be no peace for the next seventy years. The Palestinian child taught hatred from a very early age develops into the Palestinian adolescence determined to achieve 'martyrdom' in the eyes of his 'people' by the hatred-fuelled mentality whereby he wishes to kill his 'enemy' which is the Israeli or Jewish people. His religion is the 'only true' religion as he has been taught. In so far as other religions are concerned there can be no tolerance, for those who practice 'other' religions are not merely 'non believers' in the religion of Islam, but total infidels who must be wiped off the face of the earth.

Any genuine attempt to make sure that monies provided are used for the true purpose of such provision must be just that: a genuine attempt, not one which merely pays 'lip service' to the good intentions. Appropriately qualified individuals must be sent in to the schools to check on exactly what is being taught particular in relation to other cultures, religions and historical facts relevant to the area in which they live. However, it is not just at the schools that evidence has to be obtained as it is a simple matter for the school in question when aware of the attendance of an 'inspector' to falsify or at least 'water down' the relevant evidence. Individual children should be chosen at random to ascertain what they have been taught. A few families could be interviewed again with the specific objective of making certain that monies are not being used to fund the teaching of hate. That does not of course mean that alternative viewpoints are to be denied. Constructive criticism is permitted just like in many other countries. There is a world of

---

[41] Main Work. Pp. 183-195.

difference between constructive criticism, healthy debate and the one-sided teaching of hatred.

Consider a few fairly obvious and simple headline examples which could so easily be taught. The basic factual history of the land referred to by many as' Palestine' can be traced back to the early Christian era and how the area of land has changed over the years. The various historical wars concerning Jerusalem. The independent scientific/architectural evidence as to the historical existence in the land of Israelites. The period showing the rise of Islamic religion within the land. The meaning of the Ottoman Empire. The barest of outlines of the Ottoman land system and its effect upon so called the land of a forefather. The laws of conquest relating to land ownership at the time of the First World War. The doctrine of self-determination, its meaning and when it first came into existence. The basic geography of the area immediately prior to the First World War. The United Nations vote in 1947 and why such a vote was necessary. The rejection by Arab and Muslim countries of the United Nations vote and their waging of war. It is unnecessary to teach the contents of this paragraph in any form of finite detail. A brief succinct but, most importantly accurate summary, would suffice. It is not 'rocket science'.

Education, in the form of teaching essential basic history as referred to above, would however, substantially remove some of the misleading factual propaganda which has led to so much hatred. Not least of all the suggestion that the Jewish people 'stole' all the land from the Arabs or more accurately, those of the Islamic faith. It is this area, the area of the most basic education, that the eyes of those who genuinely seek peace should be turned. It is this area that the politicians should focus upon and to which consideration should be given for the imposition of all relevant sanctions in default. Ignore it and at the very least another seventy years of war and hatred awaits in consequence of which true peace is denied. It is not just the Israeli and Palestinians that this issue concerns. Anyone seeing what is happening at the present time in Syria after years of Civil War may well accept that the seeds of the next World War are likely to be sown in the Middle East. The contents of the single paragraph above provides the route to a true peace. Issues such as two states follow in consequence of these teachings. There are those in politics who believe that the resolution of the conflict lies in simply doing some sort of 'deal' involving a number of compromises and financial incentives. There is evidence that by viewing it from the perspective of a 'deal' many other disputes between nations or different groups have been resolved in the past. This situation is substantially different. The best that such a 'deal' would achieve is agreement between the various leaders sanctioned by their respective governments or parliaments. That approval is likely to lead to little more than others simply thankful as to the mere fact of such an agreement whether the agreement was one genuinely accepted by the respective peoples or not. The end result would be some form of 'peace treaty' endorsed by the respective leaders. However, there is absolutely no point in a peace treaty approved by the respective leaders or for two states if, in reality, hatred still exists amongst the people. The hatred is not there because of any 'real' injustice. It is there because of a perceived injustice which, as the facts make clear, is an erroneous and wholly unnecessary perception based mainly upon propaganda created by others.

The Settlements issue and Self-Determination

The main work dealt with this topic in the briefest possible outline. The reason for that was that it involved various complex issues which tended to detract from the principal issues with which the book was concerned. Settlements in the present context are simply areas of land which do not presently form part of the land of Israel, as recognized by the international community, for the purposes of installing or settling Israelis in such land. Much of the international community treats the relevant areas of land as forming part of the so-called 'occupied territories'. For example the 'West Bank' is described by that international community as a territory under military occupation by Israel, or Palestinian territory, occupied. In truth the overwhelming number of people who actually live there are of the Islamic faith; most referring to themselves as Palestinians. The position in Gaza is not dissimilar. It is of substantial interest to ask the question why many in the international community should adopt this descriptive approach for it is not as obvious as it would first appear. Since 2013 the ISO has adopted the name 'State of Palestine'.[42] However, the UN Security

---

[42] SO 3166-1 Newsletter V1-14 2013-02-06.

Council treats 'Palestine' as a non-sovereign entity. Accordingly this prevents it being admitted to the UN General Assembly. There are many in the international community of states, particularly those states where the majority of the citizens are of the Islamic faith, who campaign tirelessly for Palestine to be a sovereign state. However, it is an historical fact that Palestine has never been a sovereign state. There was a clear opportunity in 1947 for it to become a sovereign state. This was rejected, the waging of an aggressive war being preferred. In addition there is presently no 'true and genuine' peace. It is difficult to understand how anyone could recommend that the 'occupied territories' should be treated as a sovereign state without a real and lasting peace being established with Israel. Are there those in positions of power in the modern world who genuinely believe that by making the presently 'occupied territories' into the sovereign state of Palestine that will somehow, overnight, solve the present problem? It is just another example of the totally absurd stance adopted by many.

There had been a number of settlements in Gaza of Israelis. However, a former Prime Minister,[43] as a gesture of goodwill and in an effort to achieve peace, ordered the removal of such settlers who were then removed. As the historical evidence makes clear this did not prevent a continuing series of wars involving the Gaza Strip. A real problem with the settlement issue is that the land used for settlements is land which some members of the international community have 'earmarked' as being for a future Palestinian State. The fact that members of the international community have 'earmarked it' also literally beggars belief. It is to put the cart before the horse. It is necessary to repeat that one can't decide the issue of statehood if there is still a war, lingering with one's neighbour. Even that however is only part of the problem. The principal question which has to be answered when considering the West Bank for example, is whose land is it and why?

The reader may well be assisted by considering the Jordanian position in relation to the West Bank. The West Bank was formally annexed by Jordan on 24th April 1950. Much of the international community considered that annexation as illegal.[44] The few

---

[43] Ariel Sharon

[44] Benvenisti, Eyal (2012). *The International Law of Occupation.* Oxford University Press @p.204.

exceptions were the United Kingdom, Iraq and Pakistan.[45] Jordan subsequently transferred full citizenship rights to the residents of the West Bank and the annexation more than doubled the population of Jordan.[46] Not only did the naturalised Palestinians enjoy equal opportunities like any Jordanian citizen but they were also allocated half of the seats of the Jordanian parliament.[47] At that moment in time, incredibly, it would appear that the Palestinian problem, at least in relation to the West Bank was on the way to a possible solution. These people were no longer refugees. They had a 'homeland' with a specific nationality and with rights just like other citizens of the nation of Jordan. Unfortunately this was not to be.

In 1967[48] Jordan joined with Egypt, Syria and Iraq in waging an aggressive war against Israel. It lost that war and the West Bank fell under the control of Israel. However, at that time the Palestinians still remained Jordanian citizens. On the 31st July 1988, Jordan renounced its claims to the West Bank. (Subject to some form of religious 'guardianship' in relation to the holy sites in Jerusalem.) Subsequently, Jordan recognized the P.L.O. as the sole representative of the Palestinian people and converted the passports of those West Bank Palestinians into 'two year' travel documents. The effect was to remove their Jordanian nationality status and many of their rights which they had acquired as 'Jordanians'. There are inferences as to why Jordan had adopted such an approach, particularly in its relations to other Muslim majority countries in the Middle East, however the precise reasons are unclear. What is clear is that it is only necessary to look at a map of the region to realise how close the world came to peace

---

[45] Benvenisti, Eyal (2004). *The International Law of Occupation. Princeton University Press p.108.*

[46] Cavendish, Richard (4th. April 2000) Jordan formally annexes the West Bank" (http://www.historytoday.com/richard-cavendish/jordan-formally-annexes-west-bank) Retrieved in Wikipedia on 23rd January 2017

[47] Nils August Butenschon; Uri Davis; Manuel Sarkis Hassassian (2000). *Citizenship and the State in the Middle East; Approaches and Applications* (ttps://books.google.com/books?id=C9TkD3ugwEUC&pg=PA211lpg=P A211) Syracuse University Press. Retrieved in Wikipedia 18th October 2015.

[48] Main book P. 59

between Israel and the Palestinians by virtue of the starting point of the grant of nationality by Jordan to those in the West Bank. Of course, for those demanding a state of their own, irrespective of any absence or even possible absence of lawful entitlement, nationality of Jordan is not sufficient. Those who adopt a position leading to the compelling inference that the Palestinian approach is principally about a powerbase for rulers, as opposed to rights, fairness, or justice for the people have, in the failure of the Jordanian approach, probative evidence in support, by the following statement.

Had there not been two World Wars then the area referred to as Palestine would today almost certainly still be part of the Ottoman Empire as it was prior to the First World War. There is no evidence of any significance that those who ploughed a field, had any other occupation, or had a 'home' in the land of Palestine were rising up or would rise up to rebel against their rulers, let alone seek to kill them or their neighbours. There was no relevant suggestion of an independent state of 'Palestine' prior to World War One and the breakup of the Ottoman Empire. What clearer evidence, in addition to the numerous other matters referred to in this book, is required to prove the total absence of legal merit in the Palestinian claim. What possible relevant difference does it make if instead of being ruled by the Ottoman Empire one is ruled by the sovereign state of Jordan? They are both predominantly Muslim countries. There is no Israeli rule or any material Jewish influence.

However, there is and always has been one claim that those who claim to be Palestinian and who seek a state of their own, can properly make, yet for some reason do not appear to want to, which is this. When there are between 4 – 5 million people[49] who claim to be Palestinian who do not wish to be ruled or governed by Jordan or any Arab country let alone Israel, and wish for a state of their own then that by itself may be sufficient to invoke the doctrine of self-determination. Couple that with an area of land, which no other sovereign state can properly claim a legal right to in modern times, may also be sufficient. This has nothing whatsoever to do with ridiculous claims as to 'rights'. Neither does it have anything to do with issues such as my 'great, great uncle ploughed a field in an acre of land just here' (pointing to a dot on a

---

[49] The statistics are confusing but that figure appears to be a reasonable one from the various different statistics.

map). Equally, what promises were or were not made at the time of the two World Wars; the vote at the United Nations in 1947 all pale into insignificance by the simple genuine recognition and acceptance of being able to live in peace with ones neighbour. This in return results in Palestinians enjoying a life of 'dignity and freedom' like so many other peoples around the world which, as this Annex and the main work make clear, is in truth what one of the scales of justice demands. It is essential that such a scale is counterbalanced by the other scale of justice. The peace loving nations of the world cannot recognize a new state unless it is satisfied that the new state 'genuinely' wishes to live in peace with its neighbours and not to use it as a launching pad for yet further violence, culminating in wars of aggression against its neighbours. One only has to look at a map of the relevant area, coupled with the essential ingredient of education, to realise straight away how comparatively simple it ought to be to resolve the Israel Palestinian conflict. True it may take a couple of generations but in the time line of the Middle East this is the smallest of prices to pay for a potential real lasting peace. Again it may be necessary to repeat, this is not rocket science. It simply involves a basic recognition by those in positions of power that the approach of the multitude of statesman, politicians, diplomats, civil servants and the like have failed and failed miserably over some seventy years. These approaches have failed not because of a lack of expertise or experience or numerous other factors on behalf of the various politicians over the years. They have failed simply because of a continuing refusal to recognize that their general approach was and always has been wrong.

Consideration of other approaches and other views are not only necessary but essential by virtue of the dictates of basic common sense. Ignore it and the present situation will continue. More Israeli lives will be lost defending their homeland. Substantially more Palestinian lives will be lost by an unmeritorious claim fuelled by anger and hatred. Continuation of the present position is inconsistent with a world full of genuine statesman and wise men in positions of power, but far more consistent with that of a children's playground.

Dr. Malcolm D. Sinclair. Ph.D., LL.B. (Hons.), B.A. (Law),
Barrister. (Now retired.)